Desert Teeth

Copyright 2022 by Abalone Mountain Press
All rights reserved. Printed on Turtle Island.

Cover art by Boderra Joe

No part of this book may be used or reproduced in any manner whatsoever without the prior written permission of the copyright holder except for brief quotations in critical articles or reviews.

ISBN: 978-1-7377123-5-0

DESERT TEETH

Poems

by Boderra Joe

For my father, called to the other world
&
my family, for always sharing stories

Contents

+

Twin Lakes Haibun / 1
This House, We Gather / 2
Living with Metal / 5
America in Disguise / 8
Coffee Spoon / 17
Shimásáni Clara / 19
Belong / 21
Accelerate / 23
Black Smokey Boots / 25
Away / 27
Astro Van / 29
Some Childhood / 30

+

Fragments of Self / 34
35mm / 42
The Chosen Garden / 44
Original Heartbreak – Part 1 / 45
Original Heartbreak – Part 2 / 48
Loving You Hard / 50
The Haunting Nothing / 52
Ode to Divorce Bread / 57
To See / 59
Loop / 60

+

Yellowcake / 68
Winter in the Desert / 72
Corn Meal / 74
Hair Hangs Freely to Respect the Deceased & Spirits / 75
Chuska Peak / 78
Desert Glacier / 79
Drift, Fire, Drift, Water / 80
Rez Dog / 82
Motel Fly / 84

+

Time in the Snow / 88
Writing in General / 90
Nocturnal / 91
Tangle Teeth / 92
Indians are Everywhere in American Life / 94
Junk Poem / 97
Immolate / 98
Trade / 99
Return to Sender / 100
Lazy Lagoon / 101
Handful of Courage / 103
Belly Beast / 104
Bone-Thought / 106
Aftertaste / 111
+

Acknowledgements / 117

Twin Lakes Haibun

ice-crust dirt / kisses of water drop from sky / filling a twinned lake / mud cake dirt flicks / stains mechanical body / dark brown frosting splatters / onto rotating rubber wheels / cracks / crevices route the next rainfall / thunderclaps / the community goes black / candle sticks / some drive to the dry lake to drink / party / celebrate the invisibility to see another day / static shocks eardrums / scarring hairlines / lightning strikes power lines / metal blood soaks taste buds / power outage smokes the house / iron / propane / a whirling sack sags an empty stomach / walmart plastic bags / wave their loops to sky / water bottles whirl up in dust devils / another neighbor's trash blows onto our yard / it is snowing / it will be gone the next day / it will be muddy / take off your shoes, please / there's a car stuck in the mud below / what were they thinking / 4x4 is our life saver on the rez / the elementary school bell rings / summer lunch is the best when little / for adults, they pay or watch younglings eat / shiny bikes and pegs / low riders / we were cool to cruise around NHA housing / to the park / ride away from biting dogs / we jump dirt ramps / we smoke tobacco and talk to creator / who dumps their car seat / boxed TV / and ashes near a home / i demand an explanation

power lines tangle
black corvus crows snatch dog food
welcome to twin lakes

This House, We Gather

a womb
        a song
                a prayer
                        summer dregs

grandma's house
        we gather
                around fire
                      beneath chaha'oh

the grill
        crackles
                mutton ribs
                      achii

coffee brews
        elders heckle like hens
                near superman canyon
                      they cover their mouths

shy to show what
        little teeth they have left
                they talk of
                      herding sheep

half asleep
        a coyote
                has a leg
                      grandma loads

a shot gun
        aims and fires
                at the trickster
                      boarding school

a slow whisper
        tangled tongues
                were whipped
                        by wooden rulers

a cold whisper
        fades like smoke
                in the sharp land
                      coffee breath

dances with
        english words
                like chopping wood
                      the blade is language

english words
        taste ndn
                blood
                      for the first time

jiní
        that is what was said
                jiní
                      that was what they said
                          jiní

rez kidz
        jump laugh
                boogers crust their face
                      dry as cedar

they throw dirt
        in the air
                blessing
                      their brown faces

their thick hair
        the rest are rolling

        pulling themselves
              up on a rope

tied to a post
      down the canyon
           Shasta Black Cherry
                glistens its body

open its mouth to taste dirt
      this house
          no electricity to
              wash our hands

in a bowl of water
      dial soap on a platter
           we did not mind
              water

an imagination
     an outhouse
         where my cousin
             and i dropped a flashlight

down the pit
     in brown cake batter
         this house
             we gather

Living with Metal

shínáli pushes a rusted wheelbarrow
      leaving his shovel in front of a blast tunnel

yellow footprints adore the ground
      footprints stop before the door to enter

his wife greets his yellow powder lips
      she asks how was your day dear

while he undresses himself
      it was long he responds

he hands her his jumpsuit
      yellow dust escapes collars and pockets

never nearly comes off
      the foremen never trained nor informed

how náli should protect himself
      to protect his family

                ///

in 1940 yellow metal was discovered on Dinétah
      atomic bombs hid the sun and moon

dusty clouds enter without a sound
      Diné people wounded

exploited
      another grieving desert

cancer whispers to him
      him who hoped for lavender mornings

yellow knuckles punch the lung muckers
        punch the superiors

for late notice
        uranium can kill you

trust trust   he had
        he: a miller miner   mesa

an energy maker for arsenal
        was he not: a father husband   brother grandpa

a person
        they the takers drink clean water before him

medicine men try to heal
        cure the aches with herbs

the takers take more and more
        exchanged it for checks to Diné miners

                ///

from 1942 to 1971
        they muzzle our mouths

how do we walk in beauty
        when beauty has been taken from us

we have been mourning
        grieving in these tunnels

we sit above
        surviving on earth's fragile skin

where there is silence
        there is thunder

bold beauty embalms cedar
    stories heal wounds

from sharp landscape to songs
    replicate into poems

grief-stricken skin
    blistered eyes

possess the ghosts of past
    we rise from graves

move our bones and call it a day
    we will rise and rise

America in Disguise
for my father

in the

rearview mirror

they left

him. in

the rearview

mirror, they

left my

father

/

in 1993
a cold
black veil
covered a
family's face.
new year's
day became
a trick
a taste
of america.
that early
morning
of what
happened
and how
it was

told to
me from
my mother:
your father
was on
his way
home from
our friend's
house. he
was back
home for
the holidays.
your father
walked home
when a
visible drunk–
his two
or three
friends rinsed
themselves in
a copper
rage.
swerved.
hit.
drove away.

/

we drove

to your

nalí's house.

he wasn't

there, mom

said. her

brother shared,

his story:

i left

with his

friend to

look for

him. he

said, we

didn't know

it was

him. a

distant neighbor

heard the

thud and

called 911.

my uncle

said, i

got there.

i saw

him on

asphalt, moaning.

he was

still alive.

i grabbed

his hand

and told

him to

hang in

there.

to squeeze.

there.

there.

the ambulance

rushed town.

there.

he was

flown to

a bigger

city. there.

he took

his last

breath.

known as

a marine.

a good

man. a

good friend.

a good

son. i

call him,

late. my

late father.

/

in that
crimson morning
mirrors hid
the sun's
haunting mound.
he was

too a
devil-dog.
the cold
pushed chills
down the
spines of
the family.
blame a
name. blame
a mother.
blame an
ego. rage
spoke in
every manner.
anger never
heals a
family.

/

a devil-

dog stole

my father's

life with-

out being

in another

country.

no paper

trails were

written. the

unkind air

taped the

wounds. paid

the family

off. we

are sorry

for your

loss, here

now, a

flag to

remember him.

this america

allowed a

visible drunk

to continue

his active

duty. and

honored him

as a

good man

a good

devil-dog

when passed.

this america

camouflaged a

murderer.

/

america,
talk to
me now.
why grief
and rage
lean towards
me. nudge
my jaw.
what happened
was wrong.
this
nation and
freedom
turns to
a dead
end. no
one can
hear me
begging
for honesty

over the
booming of
the star-
spangled banner
nor the
pledge of
allegiance.
justice was
shoved in
tight throats,
red glare.
there
that day.
my father
was only
twenty-three.

Coffee Spoon
for Cora

nalí keeps the kitchen
prepares coffee
like her spoon
morning stirs our hands and feet

sunlight weaves, piles in her hair
her coffee breath hangs to dingy shades
it welcomes me
clothing my tired spine

we sat at the kitchen table
my head bows at the napkin holder
she takes notice
i dreamt of my dad, i said

she taps the mug's rim, sips
measuring life out
like her coffee spoon
slips her hand into the handle

a slanted smile appears
her lips pause at the rim
grief streams
down her face

i take hold of her hand
mourning the loss
of her son, my father
our eyes gaze at photos of him

photos that beat his memory
onto maroon walls
how our throats hold a wail
our love sighs as we flip through photos

i wish i had vivid memories of him, i said
all i have are pictures of him
holding me when i was a baby
i wish i could hear his voice just once

she nods her head
curls above her cup
sips the rim, like her spoon
stories after stories cross our hands

like her spoon she measures her life out
like her spoon she reminds me that he is still here
like her spoon it whispers, *stay, always*

Shimásání Clara

Blackberry curtains split
  gold sunrise narrow line.
    She slips on suede sandals—
    on her sandpaper soles
    as if velcro pulls away.
     Her mini steps drag
     on green carpet.
      Enter and exits bedrooms.
       She twists rods from blinds
       to illuminate rooms
       with natural light.
      Off she goes
       static feet into the kitchen
      shocking herself, fingertip
     touches radio—
    1330AM–Navajo hour
  Yéi bi chei chants rattle
  cabinet drawers.
Wooo wooo in the beginning
 tunnels the hallway.
Glass plate coffee cup
  clink onto marble countertops.
    Shimásání skates to the
    frying skillet cabinet.
     She pulls out her favorite black pan
     for bacon and eggs—
      extra crispy and sunny side.
       She glides to another counter
       bááh and potatoes wait.
        She dips her veiny hand
         into a crinkle bag of wheat bread
        where she doesn't pull out the first
       divorce bread, as she says.
      She skips that slice
     loads the toaster

            with the next.
         Másání turns away
            side-stepping into the living room
         tuning to morning news
      coffee hiccups
   next to the stainless sink
bacon, eggs sizzle on black metal,
      toaster pops up
         her not-divorce golden bread.
         Wooo wooo continues
            yolk splatters on teeth.
               She slurps creamy coffee.
               She mumbles a prayer
                  beneath her breath.
                  Glottal stopping here and there
               one hand motions in the air.
               She twiddles her thumbs
            as if she is drawing
            out her prayer.
         She sighs loudly:

hózhó náhásdlįį'
hózhó náhásdlįį'
 hózhó náhásdlįį'
  hózhó náhásdlįį'

Belong
for Nellie

On the asphalt driveway
my kindergarten teacher hands me off
to grandma.
Grandma shields the
evening light with
her right hand.
Her left wrist
bends against her hip bone.

My five-year-old
fingers crawl between
her curved fingers.
Our backs
stroke the sun.
Our shoes
press down gravel.

She limps with each step
my little feet stutter
along her side.
She grips my shoulder as a rail.
I am there
to catch her
sacrifice
my little human bones
for her brittle bones.

Her trail veins
brush my redwood cheek.
She then settles
on a velvet couch
across from me,
Where's gramma at?
"She's at work," I respond.

Nimá shá'?
"She's at work too."

Smudge window
shows off
evening haze like fire when
first started.
She holds up
her lazy brow
hobbles into
the other room.

Steps chatter
in her leave.
I lie down
on the spineless cushions.
Closing my vision
of her returning
to peck her lips
on my forehead.

Accelerate
 for Rose

My head bobbles inside a white truck traveling on gravel road.

Wheels near a turn, we pass one sheep, then two, then a flock to grandma's trailer.

Flannel shirt, boots, cowboy hat, wrangler jeans, my grandpa drops me off.

White sheetrock walls warm kitchen bodies: wood counter faces, squatting legs like grandma easing down on her chair.

Beneath the teal table, her white Hanes socks show familiar blue rez roads.

Roads, guide me up to her droopy neck. She catches my stare.

She smiles and says, "Ready?"

I nod.

Yeast breadcrumbs fall from her peach button-up shirt with a coffee stain.

My hands tuck between her arms, I lift.

Bluer rez roads reveal. I follow them on her icicle stony arms, "Jacket, ashoodí awé."

I clothe her arched back. Gather her zipper and up it went. Like wrapping a baby.

We rock side to side from gravel.
Tire crevices flick pebbles beneath metal body.

Pacing south on highway 491 to Gallup—where most of us were born.

Rubber wheels grip blacktop to incline a slant hill.

In my peripheral, grandma's bowed body jolts up and down, trying to gain power.

She switches gears, we begin to climb.

Her hand taps the dashboard, "Come on, Susie!"

Jerking herself forward, backward. We climb Tóhlakai hill.

Grandma eases herself back. Her right foot weighs down clutch.

Shift. Gas. Pedal.

Black Smokey Boots
for Sissy

horizonal mountains
flaunted her backyard
the trees, the rift—
    her thick black hair
    mirrored sadness she lugged
    vessels made by coil
        teeth made by cigarettes
        smoke pulled from sockets
        like dust thrown
            the walk down an alley
            i am doing good staying busy
            was a lie she told
        how hard it was to hold honesty in her hands
        how heavy emptiness weighed her ankles
        she swallowed darkness
    swallowed tomorrow
    the absent is real
    her loud laugh haunts me
i see a lady with a mullet
she smokes after eating
she is my auntie with another face
    i draw her face through nicotine fumes
    i say her name more than i say my own
    summer wind paused a memory
        our fishing trips, blue and silver
        stained our hands
        i knew hands could heal
            down the road by the lake
            her hands became a weapon
            to hold strong beverages
        she swallowed and swallowed
        agony drew the clouds
        like water, she escaped and passed by

	i don't smoke
	smoke quit my mouth
	the day she left
a blazed sunset
i considered a
thousand waves goodbye

Away
     for Stacie

      somewhere, she lost herself a year later
on the side i knew was a soft voice and a high laugh
with arms that could stretch and wrap you
in twine and introduce you to hip-hop then hard rock
to movies after movies, we lived off scenes
lights from the TV burned the late hours
in a house of slow love, so much love
the sound of instrumental endings echoed
the ditch behind the house
where midnight walkers roam to find shelter
or to chase their inner demons
the driveway was our basketball court
we laughed like little faces do when one says a funny thing
she was what it was like to have a big sister
and like a switch, we outgrew, and she moved away

      i'm aware, the loss of her
the house shrank, where we laid
our heads, flattened
it's not the same
a new occupant huddles her room
one that chased her to streets
and yelled to stay away
no one knew she was writing her ending
she yearned for her mother
she wrote in her journal,
i hope tomorrow is a better day, she last stated
i wept for her, i wept after her
i asked why and how and when
the pain, losing and losing a loved one after another
my window opened, the phone rang
the feeling, the second wave you get
when someone says they passed away

        at the end of each day, i reminisce
the spacious air of life we admire
the days we long to see
with windows open to create an entry
and see the horizon
to see them one last time
even if they're late
o, how i wish i could see her one last time
to listen to the new world
she stays at now

Astro Van

When we were driving   Through the valley's heat
Which lies miles and miles   Mountain, sand, wildflowers
No air conditioning   We laugh in gas station
Bathrooms while soaking   Our shirts in the sink
A slowing down for happiness   I imagine our mothers
Did not have this moment   With their parents
How enormous my mother's   Smile decorated the mirrors
Windows crank down   Summer flings herself to salty faces
They call it Death Valley   We see life
We see wings soar landscape Mom turns up the volume knob

           Another slowing down for happiness

Our mothers wake us   Pulling us to sharp water
We dip our brown feet   In a named sea
Greedy seagulls mistake   Our glittering bodies for snacks
The jaw-dropping water   Reminded us of home
How exactly this water   Stretches like dirt
Into all worlds   Bodies of dirt
Bodies of water   We slake our thirst
And thank Astro   For giving us
This slow happiness   For us

           And our mothers

Some Childhood

when i was a kid
    i remember
        catching lizards
            with bare hands
                grandma said don't touch
                    you will get warts
                        except a horned toad
                            is our relative
                        i remember
                      climbing the hills
                at Rehoboth
            with friends
          we all met at a certain
        tree close to a fence
we laughed & joked
    about silly things
        one brought a cigarette
            he lit it & inhaled it
                coughed & offered it
                    another pulled from a bush
                made his own smoke
            bush in newspaper
        he rolled it up, lit it
    smoked it up
he giggled as a response
i remember wood hauling
    cheii bought hard candy
        Shasta Cola & bologna meat filled an ice chest
            másáni always bought the newspaper
            i sat behind the seat
        in a single cab Ford truck
    eating my candy
local country singers
    sing off key hitting high notes on

                    KGAK except Vincent Craig singing *Rita*
                            a song forever taking me back to
                                wood hauling days
                                        grandma told me
                                                when i was little
                                        i'd be in the bed of
                                the truck on top of the wood pile
                        waiting for someone to buy it
                it was getting late, i said
just sell me
grandma & grandpa laughed
i remember maturing at an early age
        i, the first born
                    took care of my brothers
                        a babysitter
                            a cook   a cleaner
                            a driver   a teacher
                                    everything our
                                            mother was
                                                    while at work
                                                    i remember
                                            my late aunt's
                                    famous sun sweet tea
                            a gallon mason jar
                        tea bags brewing
                    in the summer heat
            she made sure there
was always some
at this age
        everything in place
                parts of me linger
                        as a thought to the past
                            a turned hallway of memories
                                    how easy it is to reminisce
                                            the good days

Fragments of Self

there, waiting

    in the smog world

        barbed wire separates my mother

            & i

            muddle my skeleton before her

at the margin road

        she, the one my mother calls

            sleep paralysis

        or what i call

a black gauze   soaking

            & smudging my tongue

        against charcoal wall

        i dance-wake

                a castanet rhythm, there

in the rusted corner

        the *lover*, interludes a wail

              yelling out a name, not mine

    her winter flurry skin nears

            my paralyzed body

my erasing tongue outlines her lips

        spirit bottles depend on her to open another

      smudge a prayer

          into my mouth

the dithering moon

        tethers our night

                into disagreements

                i, hold on

    to a blanket

             cold
            hungry
            tired

                in her father's home

i search for crumbs

            on scuffed floors

      she feeds manipulation

                      to another ex-ample

        i used to smile

                like the mountain

in a home

        these whiteface walls

i open each door like letters

                                    where are you?

        some days i wake to glass

                      breaking, seeing itself

broken, sharp

            my hands, a scooper

blood pieces together

                    i imagine

      this is what a heartbreak feels like

                        to mouth the word i

                                    & love
                                    & her

                        damn her

these bricks before me

            i form a bridge

                                    to pass these grinning walls

                        they judge me

critique the love

            i have for her

                                for the moon

                speaks through my bleached bones

a sunken face

        shimmers on a badge

    a divided prayer   &   beauty on meal trays

                        this place

                    i am muted

i pull out

                    my mother's words

                              from home

    who are you?

                                        another runaway

    a phase

                                        while the lover takes

                              the evening train

        out of Gallup

i am a past

                    a thought

                              as tongues carve

                my life

don't they know

                              some days i revisit

                the thin mattress

the heavy breathing behind

                        empty souls

                              skull loving mares

        listen the universe said

      you are not ready—be alive, the world needs you

your mother needs you

                          & your father is visiting

          past relatives

don't be afraid of agony

        for words are like wind

                eventually, they stop traveling

& everything stands

      still

           for a moment

                  thank the ground

for always holding you up

                & mother's spine

for always guiding you home

35mm

these sprocket twist
& load a
spool of black
& white memories

the first time
we met our
scarred knees cracked
into each other

before the
night sleeps
an illuminated face
an eyepiece reflects

shuttering poses
filters a curve
they grip hips
one eye closed

the other adjusts
shadow crows imitate
clicks as their
own aperture snaps

images stored
in one
chamber of thirty-
six i reload

my cavity to
shoot the next
hundreds to thousands
of pictures two

years together a
love so reversed
but not quite
ready what if

i process the
negatives & burn
the rolls in
a rusted barrel

bracing each portrait
landscape to enflame
souls until memories
rekindle without a

frame blocking a
square hole to
fixate each hair
strand needling a

scalp i trail
them to the
tips with my
tongue we massage

frail skin swim
on cold lips
idle into a
wash where i

strip bare thoughts
prance on taste
buds hold beneath
the radiate nail

mixing two lives
into one print

The Chosen Garden

us, in an open window
judging the world
summer air pours itself
across our lips & chests
you write the words
i love you
on my back
words diving into
skin to my spine, i
feel those
words spreading across
shoulders, you
love me like how
one loves
arcane things, complicated like
cursive writing
at least for some

our mouths
howl words
to sky
to soil beneath soles
thanks for water
and light
you carry, concealed within
i drink
slow, for the sunlight
shall dim
and a bird's tongue
licks out
tree holes and cavities
as you drew
all the nectar
from my garden

Original Heartbreak – Part 1

i looked for a place
      to sorrow
to loan my words
      beneath the opinionated sky
if allowed
      someone i used to love
is reading this
      because only faces
of those who understand
      changed you
i was there
      the nagging wind
pushed us to her room
      we shared our lips
this secret
      she was imperfect
her heavy thoughts
      statically numbed
my arm
      asleep, the stove light was on
a familiar way i was home
      mornings were still
like a cloud
      set above a mountaintop
our backs pressed against sheet
      a neighbor ignored
our messy moans
      i spent the
day-dreaming
      what if her mother
acknowledged me
      would we be a thing
those minor thoughts
      fell to feet
a choice set

        her words
red & gold
        like venom from lips
we were sewn on the same forever
        parked outside the café
my mother knows about us & your past
        my past
grew legs one summer
        it whispered in her mother's ears
who can forget a past like mine
        one that left me in scattered pieces
on empty shelves
        a person like her
mother chewed &
        dissolved my worth
i no longer handled
        risky sadness
i want to grow old with a man
        she sang afar
my eyes rolled
        to my shoulder
was i an example
        i drove miles
& believed warmth was still there
        we shared our bodies
our run-on sentences
        at a hotel
in a town that forbidden us
        to love & hold
sweat & love
        no complaint
was an answer
        we collided at hips
stretched our joints
        sampled each other's longing tongue
it meant something
        what goes up comes down
fast & hard

       she, the aggressive lover at night
grinded the waves
       fended each second
by day, she
       a religious walker forgot my name
forgot the words behind my teeth
       forgot the space between
for the ground dropped
       fast & hard

Original Heartbreak – Part 2

      in an infinite tunnel
a church spoke in bread
      from her mother's alter
she begged me to leave her offspring
      in mother's dark
corner she hid a man's sin
      for years
it turned wine into guilt
      shame watched her sleep
but our love proceeded
      i, a scribbled name
she tried removing
      with vinegar
she ate the apple
      and got a treat
the forbiddenness it took
      for her to not reach
i gathered reasons
      i couldn't let go
& why i should
      the apple-seeds planted
in that love
      hard and unforgiving
the heart like a fist
      a punch to love
out of me
      forget my face
love, an expectable word
      a word i couldn't correct
how strange that was yet
      i crossed her path
did you really love me, she asked

        yes i mean i did
how my fingers typed
        & sent with a pause
yes i did love her
        but i let go
because the love
        did not age like wine
i wanted her
        in my throat in my mouth
at all times
        but she did not want
someone like me
        she wanted some
other somebody
        holding her
like binds that hold
        god's words
i removed
        the petals from her name
and drank the wine
        at my door
i don't like wine
        but it was
her way letting me taste her
        bitter and grief

Loving You Hard

no one loves you more
      than salted tongues
proposing the right words
      in the next stride
i, waiting
      you don't want to know
what i'm really thinking
      teeth claw & clench
don't worry
      is a lie we tell ourselves
loving someone hard
      can be dangerous
one day they wake up
      leave
or stay
      like dusty books
with their unread pages
      and unvisited worlds
what happened to our love
      did we consume
did we forget that it's us
      knowing you
and your thoughts
      i am worthy
i am here
      loving you hard
sheds the skin for healing
      was it my fault
that i didn't consider
      does it matter
you are there
      piece by piece
the people i know
      work together in mud
they attach themselves

       move forward together, a rhythm
like a train
       to move on track
needing its coal
       just like i need you
my eager self
       delayed

The Haunting Nothing

blood pools to the cheek

    these walls are bones

        these pipes are veins

                we're all stories

            in the end

        the face

the one in clouds

    the one on wallpaper

        did you know eyeballs can melt

                in a fire

            if it's the right kind of fire

        runny eggs on black skin

the face, i see it again

    on the wallpaper, in the dark

        melted eyes running

                down cheeks

            leaning on a habit

            leaning into a habit

trying to rid away habits

      but habits pull you further away

           there is not enough

                                        space

                                  nor pages

                            for all my skin

talking low to a suitor

      the dark nothing

           i feel nothing

                                  i can't feel any-thing

                        this black hole of no-thing

                  floating

is this what death feels like

      numbness

           alone

                                  nothing

                          what if it's like that

                      when we die

to be alone

    feel nothing

        when my father died

                i made it rain rocks

            stupid and hungry are brothers

        fear and guilt are sisters

the scratches behind walls

    are mistaken for rats

        time isn't a line

                nor dominoes

            as i thought

        were beginning & end

moments fall around me

    like snow

        rain

                confetti

        this house is like a body

      it has eyes

bones

    face

        skin

                          this room

                    is like the heart

                no, the stomach

of the house

    it puts on different faces

        while it slowly digests

                        my sanity

              why do i feel nothing

          monsters are tiny little

movements inside me

    scattered into so many

        pieces like new snow

                          or confetti

                forgiveness

            i see its face

    in clouds

        in water

            in mud

                              it's warm like a tear

                      on the cheek

            i fear

Ode to Divorce Bread

You,
divorce bread,
you sit,
at every beginning,
end,
of loaf.
Dry hands
skip your rise,
from flour.
Square or round,
you multiply
from mother's rolls.
How simple
yet complex
to not devour,
to spread peanut-butter,
grape jam,
across your face.
Grandma said
to not eat you.
You will
ruin my marriage,
or ignite a fire
in a pit for lurking
spirits to cast upon me.
But, there you are,
waiting–
molding blue,
growing like
thighs, breasts, mouths,
fire and seeds.
You, expand,
at the right temperature,
edges soften.
There, always

two of you at every
beginning and end.
O bread,
you let me
toast your length,
hold your
wheat fingers.
Sea and soil
gaze at your
golden crust.
Give me your
daily self.
I will not dare
marry,
to be married
to you,
and only you.
Let me wrap
your bread shoulders,
kiss me with
your dough lips,
be my beginning
of each end.
My divorce bread,
lover.

To See
    after Richard Siken

moonlight spills, soaking our layers our onyx-selves

      silver tongue on the marble floor

the sunrise snaps the bones of our lungs

      like pinecones under your feet

it is a surprise to us

      the living-room shades black as veil

          the starlight pounds us in a fist of buckled knees

we lift our palms to our faces as if

      to shelter it, our bloody knuckles dry as black-ash midnight

      flooding into our chalked bones

we are tiny closets packed in shoe boxes

      with strands of string slinking, slithering, sliding

the pearl glow is no secret

      white pearl: a thing to retain the moon

          from escaping itself

Loop

                                        tick

tick   *merry-go-round around a round*   tick

                                clicking tongue wooden blades

tick   tick

                                        tick

night *e x h a l e s*

        glimmers

                its soul

                        hangs itself

                                for the next

                                          igniting day

flick

flash

slander

town

high

beams

orange

flame

corners

repeat repeat

right   right   left   left distinctly

        coyotes scream

                like hyenas

                        beside a well

              ~~tangle~~ tails

      ring around

sagebrush

veiling	grim
drapes	above
flooded	adobe
roofs	mirroring
mirroring	eight
eight	eight
eight	eight
eight	eight
eight	legs
tour	across
ocean	sky

cursive limbs

blinking | loose cables

tap vein   lids hum

around red   bone lines

weary sn00ze   wake up

Yellowcake

amber minerals
swirl and

tunnels shi-
nálí's throat

for thirst
his yellow

dough hands
hugged together

for biscuits
a scratched

windpipe elapsed
overtime he

coughs sore
for green

paper limbs
loose change

swap his
lungs and

kidneys clog
with mucus

the livestock
graze extra

parts running
fingers through

fur missing
hair his

hair yellow
yellowtails sink

and suckle
on red

blood cells
lemon crumbs

seep through
his window

screen split
wood walls

we are here

gold mine
water spills

San Juan
river flaxen

fish gills
crayola yellow

poison in
soil rotting

corn squash
sinkholes on

Diné reservations
yellow green

cesspools flood
shináli's home

floods my
aunt's breast

inhaling dust
exhaling chemo

yellow clouds
fuss behind

Church Rock
residents enrage

our people
are seized

fenced by
cancerous filth

five hundred
abandon mines

took and
takes

more burials
wooden canes

velvet shirts
floral skirts

sweep and
vacuum royal

yellow from
sheetrock to

jumpsuits and
leather boots

lemon-crumbs
curl in

my aunt's
bed slithering

on silk
pillows cradling

gold eyes
for hope

goodnight gold
blink sleep

Winter in the Desert

we tell ourselves
dry in our voice
      shadows agitate the night
      tumbleweeds twist the
fence lines alongside dirt roads
we walk on
      listening to Yéi bi chei hymns
      on the reservation
in this world
the fourth world
      inside our homes
      light and warmth

it falls white outside on bone branches
we listen hear only the snaps of wood
      between cedar wood crackles
      grandma speaks

            listen to the earth she speaks in
                  wind rain snow

we tell ourselves
dry in our voice
      what we know is nothing
      but the tune of our bones
the chants and prayers we sing
are for those below, above
      and around us that we
      listen beyond the fireplace
for when we rest at night
above other worlds
      we will greet new mornings
      finding ourselves
in the limbs of loved ones
as our elders would say

> *your loved ones are*
> *cold   hungry   tired*
> *build a fire   cook   make a bed*

in this world
grandma said between fire crackles
    we sit at our homes
    cold wind rushes against hooghans
pass the dogs' ears
coyotes yelp to the glitter moon
    their misty breaths gather stars
    wild burr tangle with tails

> *listen to the earth*
> *she howls growls roars*

buzzards cackle at them
when trying to cross highways
    we tell ourselves
    dry in our voice
we exist because of our stories
that nothing is as lucid
    as a rattlesnake's tail
    in the middle of winter
that horned toad is our cheii
we come from more

> *listen to the earth*
> *she speaks*

grandma said
walk on
    listen for a voice
    in this world

Corn Meal

early spring morning, wind
hands-over blessings to
mother earth's mouth, a
low prayer nudges at

corn husks, the eastern
sun dances above lilac
mountains, she holds a
jar close to the

tassels to dust off
pollen to offer a
prayer of any sort
a yellow pinch releases

on her Diné tongue
the sweetness melts, rests
on top of her
head and returns to

mother's roots, a prayer
is drawn in sand
blowing bush waves up
to the sun's burning lips

Hair Hangs Freely to Respect the Deceased & Spirits

there is my tongue
near the ground
it releases dust
and history
silence and desert's
lips welcome me

        over there

                loud cemeteries
                linger with bones
                in curiosity
                grave cells and time
                shift in language
                livers and lungs
                drown in dirt

night

    air interrupts
    a whisper down the hall
    the journey to your bed
    on your knees
    your hands
    clasp together
    prayers flick streetlights

        like a growl

                where there are
                no mutts
                like shoes with
                no soles in them
                like a dress with
                no woman
                like a shout
                no tongue or throat

along

        blue waves
        staining white
        on a cliff
        like heat chanting
        and crackling
        firewood in a stove
        in grandma's hooghan

                like a dress

                        on a broom
                        thick threads
                        brushing for
                        crumbs
                        searching for
                        life

like telling clocks

        a metaphor of
        how fast and
        short we live
        make use of a
        good night sleep
        give immediately to children's faces
        when they tug at clothes
        holding wonder
        like a cup

                for the years

                        of loss
                        and war
                        bends our
                        knees

                                    once about
                                    a house
                                    in fear-
                                    ful hands
                                    an imagin-
                                    ation

let's revisit

                    pine trees
                    the eyes that love you
                    arms grasping
                    your memories that
                    star the night
                    accompanied
                    by a song

Chuska Peak

                    each day i look north. i stare at his rocky skull.
      tracing his thoughts like back roads. dust blows and mutely lays on his water washes. sun baked rocks stretch to other chapter houses. wind lifts lake water, creating a rainbow mist for children's faces. even the sun loves its reflection. i have been here plenty. my breath hangs like a cloud on his peaks. i leave behind written poems about worth, fearlessness, and chaos, versions of myself for my family. his boulders are like rough shoulders dipping in streams. he went through so much, so let's be gentle. he was on fire and i know he was raging. his silence was a threat to his enemies. it seems our own silence can be one too. his rock hands dig for relief for hunger. to offer medicine to those that tried to burn his purpose. he is worn but not beaten. sun and frost and fire cannot erase history. warriors shake his soul by yelling off cliffs. how much forgiveness wasn't a hesitation.

Desert Glacier

1. cold wind
brews and whirls
lifting grains
of sand
to tiny dust devils

2. clouds break forth
streams of light
flare through
brownish
fractured bottles

3. red maroon slogans
splash souls
on rock faces
smearing the
purity of earth

4. singers of dawn
inspire the shadows
above mountains
between cracks
through low caves

5. gathering one small
nest on top
a desert glacier
brooding wings droop
in living spring

6. in shades speak
stories of past
to teach us humans
how to last to fight
against greed

7. how dare they
disturb her?
how dare they abuse
her by trash writing
across the land?

Drift, Fire, Drift, Water

in abalone
      mountains dress themselves
      cuff their wrist
      in turquoise gems
      gaspeite hangs
      from necks
      she is ready to rebel

mountains slander
      their lips
      glide with sky
      a neighbor
      she is drilled for tunnels
      releasing ash coal
      she coughs black
      and bedazzled jewels

outsiders swindle her
      greed looks like coins
      while standing on her
      yanking courage
      from her teeth

soaring breasts
      wings and beaks
      rulers of the woods
      scratch their backs
      on stumps
      tiny creatures
      hide in openings
      chewing green leaves
      what seems to be their last meal

workers like axes
        crop trees
        lock their jaws
        grind stumps
        receding hairlines
        of homelands

hold on to
        what's left of water
        in the driest season
        hands rough
        dry patches
        maps reveal
        faces to
        where rivers flow
        where meals were
        prepared for gathers

they are thirsty
        behold oil spills
        they are thirsty
        black and yellow
        gushing gold
        mining water
        they are thirsty

to drink brown water
        as our ancestors did
        you would call it bravery
        i call it black-market
        for the bare of me
        these delicate lines
        frighten me

Rez Dog

it's summer

      moths scan
      fuse light

hypnotized
by porchlight

      into dog's mouth
      a cotton appetizer

tunnel water
an aftertaste fur legs

      like scab wounds
      on dog's torn ear

matted fur sheds
off its body

      knots onto
      loose-nails

string light
attracts beady eyes

      on the back
      moth's fur jacket

this dog
snaps its jaw

      its teeth
      snaps in the

summer's eve
for more

    and more
    this dog survives

dangerously, it faces
trucks head-on

Motel Fly

a fly
poses on the dreary curtains
in motel 6
it kneels and warms its hands
like i do when in winter
its red compound eyes
poor vision
tries to make the drink i drink
from a red can with a poled straw
antennas steer to smell
lands atop sugary fluid
vomits juice
to absorb liquids
because flies do not have teeth

lethal footprints taste sweet
fly papers
a slow sticky death
ultraviolent light
show where there is life
there is a grey body
with four dark stripes on its back
its lonely wings–
halts a balanced flight
veiny wings dance
two-hundred times per second
during the day
zero at night
this goddamn
fly—smoking
the fumes
left by previous
visitors

Time in the Snow

five
in the morning
i awake
                        with brilliance of
                            streetlights
                            my ash knees
                                                  shield my heart
                                                  those dirt roads
                                                  graded by tractor

grading the past
to smooth a path
for hard times
                        i have a hard time
                        sleeping and waking
                        pulsing red numbers
                                                  give meaning
                                                  to my room
                                                  to my life

every sixty seconds
i listen to the wind
which is about to
                        tell me a secret
                        but doesn't
                        i keep listening
                                                  my head
                                                  against the wall
                                                  against the floor

when grief
pours many bones
into the ground
                        two hundred six
                        or so
                        i can see

                                        the yawning light
                                        how midnight blue
                                        is there for a second

hunger for day
hills after hills
light consoles in clothes

                        snowflakes
                        gather our bones
                        clean and shine

                                        rest down on
                                        wooden steps
                                        on parked vehicles

streetlights dim
smoke from the
fireplace

                        the wind carries
                        my mother
                        rises from her bed

                                        walks through corridor
                                        where light greets
                                        her fire lips

it was then
i wanted to
crawl back to

                        mother's womb
                        to remember warmth
                        and history

                                        my mother
                                        ageless like rock
                                        fraying her love

across the desert field
up to wild crows
love melted the snow

Writing in General

you are writing
                fingers cramp
                              a glitch
                                            thoughts gurgle its

breath
        past tense
                and self-worth
                          whether you're ahead

at least try and see
                where silence
                          takes you
                                    maybe to lakes or roads

we drift away
                and don't notice
                          until we reflect
                                  it's okay to be the

blank page
        you can add to it later
                        it's good
                              to let your thoughts roam

on their own
            let your words
                      pat the land
                              and stay forever

Nocturnal

      i approach sleep: confront its night soul
thoughts mingle with pain
darkness etches itself on walls
making itself at home in the corner
even streetlights could stretch so far
darkness could be a good thing
we came from darkness when we were born
      the house talks and it talks too much
secrets fling onto those who
walk through the east door
they are messengers
word gets around
about the darkness beneath a roof
but darkness could mean a good thing
      our eyes adjust to darkness
we become the darkness
our bodies deliver darkness
our thoughts bring shadows
darkness is eager and needy
it wants to be seen
to see the first light
on its palms
and say this is nice
we welcome darkness
and not mistake
its teeth for fear
but a smile
      darkness starts inside
and needs no permission
to enter as we sometimes
block out light
and darkness takes that
as a welcoming
even when our eyes
close for the night

Tangle Teeth

the sound of teeth cracking
is unbearable
    like a bilagáana saying:
    We birthed a nation from nothing
he meant to say:
We stole and killed and killed Natives for everything
    silver skin flash
    their Indian jewelry
I love Indian jewelry
they say while refusing service
    to a familiar face:
    hunger and thirsty
i have dreams
losing a tooth
    or many
    like my identity
to be erased
because fear
    because i exist
    from mountains
to water
along my bloodline
    along these words
    written before me
my people
write their own stories
    not you or them
    cavities in land
linger—colonization
the thought
    of a tooth pulled
    from my head
thrown into a mason
jar to collect dust

        that is what has been done
        a collection of bones
show them off and note
"Real authentic Native bones"
        you pour my remains
        onto your palm to feel
some sort of sacredness
when blood at hands
        it is washed away
        whereas, i lick my wounds
rattle my bones
in your closed fist
        listen to them
        i am here
clink them together like a rock
i speak stories
        my bones
        my gums
roll and align
my tongue

Indians are everywhere in American life
      –Various curators in the National Museum of the
      American Indian

We are here, though, we are discussed
in third person
as if we are not standing in front of you
Once again, we are removed
relocated, replaced with a single word
they–
went through so much
they–
are everywhere

You tape our mouths and correct our history
You teach us about gore and damage
and say they don't exist
You raise your right-hand from your side
shape an O with your mouth—
your open palm
disrupts the
O / o / O / o

Indians are everywhere in American life
Indians are everywhere
We spot each other out
in cities from east to west to the north
and down to the desert
We nod at each other
whisper, "Look, a Native"
and offer a handshake
share Hello's in our language
and Goodbye's in agony

You say our language is violent
We say language mends—
our tongue licks gold walls, taste white bearings

the naked murals envy our brown skin
Our brown imagination
demands there be more of us
More to taste decision
Look at the high ceilings
Look in the largest library
Look up Indigenous history
American, American life is everywhere

Again, we are here
We are here
Our bones taste like sweet corn
You ask if we are free or NDN
We are here
We are here
We feed and bleed for
the land you stand on—
we offer our handrail spines
and corn pollen
We burn
burn cedar or sage.
Smoke coils to mountains
to cities, to the capital walls
Behind dirty glass
You point and point
fingers against glass
Look, look, that's how an NDN looks
You take a photo of our ancestors
And post on your social media
Hashtag woke, hashtag Indians

Our relatives always say, don't bite the hand that feeds you
Bite the hand that starves you
We detach your fingers
unfold the skin
remove the bones
place them in a jar, note, real authentic white bones
sell them at gas stations—

by dreamcatchers and gluten free treats
Store owners follow and stare
at our long hair
They stare when we eat
They stare and ask, "What is it like to live
on the reservation?"
We can afford to be here
To talk business
To teach our history
To walk next to briefcase heads
and suited fellows
We are pulled away
from our belly that
birthed us
Though, we are here
We are here

Junk Poem

    A poem appears. The poem grips & junk appears. *Junk*—a word to describe a thing, a place, a person. We are made of everything & everything is made of us—does that mean if this poem is a waste, trash, debris it makes me a junkie poet? A mattress is time spent by loved ones—they touch, kiss, & hold each other questioning life. Throwing it away & considering it to be junk, does that mean the ones that laid their heads on the mattress are a waste of space? I assume the splinter door is another junk that once blocked & hid impulses & pressing fists. Look at the sandy beer bottles, a common being—it numbs your bones & marrows & teeth & it emits spiraling truths. Drink its body once, twice, maybe for the rest of our lives, we lose something. Keep searching this ditch. This whole mess travels like flies, it mitigates here & there on the rez. Most of these are savable. The creator created artists, we create worlds like coffee grounds, mountain tops, hummingbirds, jewelry, handmade. Real, real work, no negotiation. I look hard & see used tires. Grandpa would put them to use. It will hum his ride & maybe then he can drive & drive & pickup his grandkids & wife. Torn fur & webbing bones & maggot flesh, they spill to the center, growing—now that is colonizers feeding off our carcass. They take a huge chunk of our stomach claim it as theirs, a bag of jewels. If mother could speak she would swallow them whole & spit them out to the ocean's mouth, they were better off at sea, probably start another war & claim the waters. This ditch smells of rotten potatoes & blooming lilies. What a word to describe everything too, ditch & pit, both are a cavity no one wants to treat, to let it rot & bleed. Oftentimes, past lovers ditched us, threw us in a pit to bury ourselves alive. If that taught us anything, we live in a world that teaches us to fight. This pandemic ditch—lost jobs, lost homes, inflation, raised ego banks. When retaliating, a considered threat. They rattle our sanity. See for yourself the "junk" they left for us to buy, build a wealth. To break our backs & fuel our throats. We don't lack meaning.

Immolate

a simple light enflames

tarry liquids linger around members

something is left

more than ash

more than black sand

a soul worth saving

a face worth touching

a smile worth seeing

skin exhales smoke

bones are left as an offering

emancipation the spirit

a starved flame

feast

and feast

Trade

we look a bit ill
do you ever wonder why?
my people are seen as
brown drinkers
our faces and names
fade like tin cans
in the desert sun
we can change that
it was a trade
we want ourselves back
and return your drink
i have watched what it could do
it has taken my relatives
it has power because you
gave it power to rid us
i, too, had my share
i, too, lost myself
to numb the taste of moments
a tragic to die with a bottle in one hand
and the other to bury our relatives
back into mother's womb
we call this trauma and murder

Return to Sender

america
what's your address
can you prove it?

        i have no physical address
        a PO box will do
        i live on the rez
        i must travel to a post office
        i have to prove my location
        i have to draw a map of my home
        to renew my ID
        america made us relocate
        forced us to walk, very far
        america bought their address
        bought the homes we were supposed
        to live

Lazy Lagoon

        moonlight breaks shimmer waters
    water beads
        the things, the many things of light
            a sickness tides the shore
        flashes its teeth
          engage its soul
              in days, body chills
        night sweats with candles
          between thighs
              three tests: positive

candles show its wax
    dawn breaks behind
        ill eyes
            from skull to toes
      the wind, the bloody wind
    light a sky
        if hands were sanitized
          my words behind mask
      wipe the bones
      wipe the oil tears
        slide on the waters
            wash my hands
            wash my face

            stay away from loved ones
              sleep separate
          eat alone
    talk to the door
        wait for an answer
   walk the symptoms
      tie it to a leash
          ache constantly for a touch–
              a kiss
              a voice

                    help distract a fatigued brain
                        lose taste
                                lose smell
                                        lose a thought

                                i am weak
                            bones are sap
                    stick to water muscles
                        sand cramps
                            i wonder how my family is doing
    isolate

                            blood jumps to moonlight
                                light breaks the night
                    secret soil growls
                                through sockets
                            afternoon halts
                                a love fog,
                    pray on hillside shoulders
                            pale water
        in the next room
                            dark alone
                    maybe mother's breast
                            mother's tender love
            can unhinge this cloudy slain
                                i pray to rid
                        this blaze and bloom
                                    light the candle
                and blow away meadow air
                                blow to the stars
                    don't let the ripple spread

Handful of Courage

let us go
    to spark a match for warmth and existence
let us go
    to block the roads to protect our east entrance from
    drunken drivers
let us go
    to shield our grandmothers, mothers, and sisters from
    tempered fists
let us go
    and bloom into abalone thoughts
let us go
    and shower our core in coral mornings
let us go
    and strengthen our native tongue with glottal stops
let us go
    hum in sync a rhythm to shut those lying numbers up
let us go
    and transform lies, *All Natives are dumb, stupid and*
    alcoholics
let us go
    and rewrite the system to secure honor and find our
    missing relatives
let us go
    and barricade our homelands from violence – from
    tear gas, from rubber bullets,
    from batons—they spit on our dirt and expect respect
let us go
    and pray-sing in our own resilience
let us go
    and walk our own beauty with feet as water and poems
    in hand
let us go
    and do what we do best, exist

Belly Beast

here we are
        at what this piece of country hands us

      a heavy universe
by last year's end

add salt like sorrow
        to burning forests

                add hope to those decaying
                into soil, boneless

these words don't taste good
        like a run-on sentence
a spoiled diary

            we must sing our songs
            take back *our* stories

no status could revise rage
        against eyes flashing thieves
        & pockets burning

                so, look to the sky
                & rise like a wave

            this is how we will surpass
      crash down hard
            on other beasts' bellies

abalone moon speaks light
        hard like a yellow bolt

                this is our time
            like yesterday & the day before

they say our language is violent
    read that again

        they say our language is violent

          the belly beast
              has awakened

Bone-Thought

my grandma's kneecaps smile during the day then frown at night

my mother snores loud, a way of her bragging that she's the reason i am here

because of her my voice echoes and returns

in the dark i can see the light that first birthed me

sunrise and sunset lie together like sweethearts to create a horizon

life is precious but fragile when grieving

and having a little more is plenty

i'm caught between holding my place or keeping my peace

to question ambiguity and the silence between response and none

and forgiving is never forgetting and that letting go is never easy

and being lost is a four-letter word but so is hope

which both have a hint of wonder

to speak clearly and say this is what i believe

i am seen as a threat with my brown skin and brown words

how i blend so well with the ground i walk

that i am followed and stared at in many places

and yes, that happens daily

how correcting my english is their way of minimizing my voice

i write and speak in Diné bizaad of what i know

silence is mistaken for peace and not mutiny

this space, i align to recollect myself

sometimes my past likes to reminisce and confuse me

i was told, i feel nothing towards you at all and never will

but asked if i still love them and if i was with someone

you hear the confusion

beauty can deceive itself with tongue and vision

i prefer real and honest even if it means i am not ready

am i ever ready

am i ever prepared for the unexpected

i lost an aunt—she was homeless and sick

i did not know

her daughter, my cousin, followed her

she too became sick from grieving her mother

that is foreshadowing well done

do i have all the time in the world

i haven't slept the same among the words that a person left for me

to lay in bed with her words tucked beneath my pillow

what does she mean by this

i love her without knowing where it comes from

or how or when or why

as we all love someone directly

with problems and pride

what makes a person fast: adrenaline and lies

maybe i prefer to live this life

where i have only these words to offer

and no change to spare i am home

rich in books rich in words

you speak poor english one said to me

you write in poor english too

i write read and speak what i hear

what i see and how i see it

if poor is what you are aiming for

please tell me in your pale words

then i will say you speak with hate

and you bash the poor and bash

people like me

i am alone like this line

like this poem

maybe i don't fully understand myself

the bones that hold my spine

the muscles that talk to my brain

are what fascinate me

how communication isn't the same as comprehension

that a bull and lion aren't compatible but their hearts

are made of dirt and fire—sandstone

tell me how i am overqualified

tell me why you ask for my desire

and budget my needs

was i a diverse hire

you don't have enough experience

credit hours don't count as experience

tuition don't count as experience

a higher degree don't count as experience

being alive don't count as experience

how am i ever supposed to learn

you can train me

on what exactly

how not to be brown

how not to react to racial slurs

how not to be too NDN

Aftertaste

i am brown
      raised straight from dirt
where too my mother and father came about
      where my placenta is buried
alongside siblings outside our grandma's home
      pass Tóhlakai then Twin Lakes

                                                  this is home

i am bilingual
      shiłnilí i respect the dirt
whirling its back behind grandpa's truck
      the yadilah from grandma's bedroom
circling wrong letters from word search
      gold beams pass through shutters
floorboards cry below soles with each flux
      rez dogs chase, bark
at indigo shapeshifters
      cedar embers light our faces
we caress pearl river haze onto our toes
      our heads and heart
a melody prayer courses around aluminum

                                          this is language

i am resilient
      my eyes flash like coal in fire
driving on gutted roads
      highway 491—the devil's highway
where darkened beer bodies blink in sunlight
      a drunk driver
runs over my father on new year's day
      from the devil's highway to gallup—
drunktown crossing over the border town
      into the unknown fear—fear has blades

will i return home safely
      will the drunken day drinkers stay home
or stagger off spinal-column-tracks
      the train's horn separates   my aunt   my cousin
their hands cup vodka bliss in bars or bootleggers
      licking their wounded livers
a weathered disease
      to be injured or to repair itself
                                         this is the aftertaste

Acknowledgments

I extend my gratitude to the following publications and their teams for publishing versions of these poems: *Tribal College Journal, Yellow Medicine Review, Mass Poetry,* and *New Mexico Poetry Anthology.* Thank you for offering me space.

Ahxéhee' to my late father, Derrick Joe, Sr. for you're missed dearly and for the person you were while you were here, your legacy lives on. This book is dedicated to him.

To my mother, Geraldine Casuse, for your unconditional love, support, and strength. You're my pride! To my brothers, Derrick Jor, Jr., Eyan Tsosie, and Talon Tsosie, you each hold a special place in my heart for your humor, love, and support.

To my whole family, especially shimásáni Clara Casuse and shinálí Cora Joe, for your stories and prayers have taught me to listen and observe. I thank my cousins, aunts, and uncles that have shared and continue to share their laughter with me.

I thank my friends, for always checking in on me, loving me, and supporting me in many ways possible. You're all a blessing!

To my mentors: Sherwin Bitsui, Joan Naviyuk Kane, and Santee Frazier, for all your words of encouragment, guidance, and friendship throughout this book's journey. And to the Institute of American Indian Arts low-residency MFA program for offering a space for Native voices.

Ahxéhee' to all those that have shaped and shared their wisdom with me by the following writers, educators, mentors, scholars, organizers: másáni Esther Yazzie-Lewis, Manny Loley, Amber McCrary, Luci Tapahonso, Layli Long Soldier,

Jon Davis, James Thomas Stevens, Evelina Lucero, Orlando White, Kimberly Blaeser, Jennifer Foerster, and Byron Aspaas.

A huge ahxéhee' to you, readers, for supporting this book and reading each line. I hope these poems walk away with you and offer some fragments of beauty.

Boderra Joe is a Diné poet, journalist, and photographer from Bááhazł'ah (Twin Lakes), New Mexico, on the Navajo Nation. She is Bit'ahnii (Folded Arms Clan), born for Tabááha (Water's Edge Clan). She holds an MFA and BFA from the Institute of American Indian Arts. She is the recipient of the Willapa Bay AiR Fellowship, the Indigenous Nations Poets (In-Na-Po) Fellowship, and the Bosque Redondo Memorial Artist-In-Their Residence Fellowship.

www.ingramcontent.com/pod-product-compliance
Lightning Source LLC
Chambersburg PA
CBHW030040100526
44590CB00011B/278